ARE YOU STRESSED?

CHILL OUT

We've got you covered. Or should I say colored? Relax… unwind and have a good laugh as you color in these hilarious farting frogs.

FREDDY THE FARTING FROG

FROM TINA VO

FREDDY THE FARTING FROG

FROM TINA VO

follow us on Instagram
@shoptinacompany
and don't forget to leave us a
review on our Amazon Product Page.
Happy coloring!

FREDDY THE FARTING FROG

FROM TINA VO

FREDDY THE FARTING FROG

FROM TINA VO

FREDDY THE FARTING FROG

FROM TINA VO

FREDDY THE FARTING FROG

FROM TINA VO

FREDDY THE FARTING FROG

FROM TINA VO

FREDDY THE FARTING FROG

FROM TINA VO

FREDDY THE FARTING FROG

FROM TINA VO

FREDDY THE FARTING FROG

FROM TINA VO

FREDDY THE FARTING FROG

FROM TINA VO

FREDDY THE FARTING FROG

FROM TINA VO

FREDDY THE FARTING FROG

FROM TINA VO

FREDDY THE FARTING FROG

FROM TINA VO

FREDDY THE FARTING FROG

FROM TINA VO

FREDDY THE FARTING FROG

FROM TINA VO

FREDDY THE FARTING FROG

FROM TINA VO

FREDDY THE FARTING FROG

FROM TINA VO

FREDDY THE FARTING FROG

FROM TINA VO

FREDDY THE FARTING FROG

FROM TINA VO

FREDDY THE FARTING FROG

FROM TINA VO

FREDDY THE
FARTING FROG

FROM TINA VO

FREDDY THE FARTING FROG

FROM TINA VO

FREDDY THE
FARTING FROG

FROM TINA VO

FREDDY THE FARTING FROG

FROM TINA VO

FREDDY THE FARTING FROG

FROM TINA VO

FREDDY THE FARTING FROG

FROM TINA VO

**Don't forget to follow us on Instagram @shoptinacompany
and don't forget to leave us a review on our Amazon Product Page. Happy coloring!**

FREDDY THE FARTING FROG

FROM TINA VO